Teacher's Edition

QUIZ 'N COLOR PAGES

Supplemental Teachers' Guide to
The Alphabet Bible Characters
Volumes 1 • 2 • 3

PLEASE NOTE

This is a Teachers' resource book **ONLY**.
Permission is granted by the authors to reproduce these
pages by copier for non-commercial classroom use only.
DO NOT color the pages or write in the quiz answers in this
volume or write in the quiz answers or copying from
your Master will not be possible.

Purpose and Description of this Book

As a supplement and study aid to the *Alphabet Bible Characters Volumes 1 - 3*
this book contains, in order:

• Table of contents to locate all characters.

• Alphabetical arrangement of characters divided in order from all three volumes of the Alphabet Bible

Characters books. (Total of 78 lessons)

• Coloring sheet of main character, often with supporting cast.

• Bible character's descriptive verse

• Quiz questions with word scramble clues. The answer requires the child or teacher to carefully read the

Bible character's descriptive verse.

• Final quiz question that identifies the symbol reminder of the character.

• Answer page located in back of book.

Bible character's descriptive verse from:
The New Revised Standard Version Bible,
Copyright © 1989 National Council of the Churches of Christ in the USA.
(Used by permission.)

Why do we use Rhymes?

• Children learn and remember best from games and the easiest and most basic game is learning by heart a simple and often humorous rhyme. We are deliberate in encouraging young readers to memorize these little narratives that reveal the essence of each of these characters. This valuable information will stay with them the rest of their lives.

• The 21st Century is a good place to begin replacing the now- meaningless medieval- origin- Mother Goose Rhymes with something more substantial and with actual teaching value. Most of the nursery standards are actually about events like the Bubonic Plague (Ring Around the Rosie) and countless forgotten kings, queens and political leaders (Mary, Mary, Quite Contrary was England's Bloody Mary; Little Boy Blue was Cardinal Thomas Wolsey; Humpty Dumpty was a canon, etc.) The rhymes in our collection celebrate familiar Bible figures, each with a precise story that is worthy to remember. They are straightforward and biblically accurate and will never be demoted to nonsense from a forgotten era.

What is Our Theology?

• We have chosen Bible characters that are the best representatives of role model qualities children can follow. Examples:
  ○ Abraham models Faith. (Genesis 11)
  ○ Abigail models hospitality to strangers. (1 Samuel 25-30)
  ○ Cornelius exemplifies Love Your Enemies (Acts 10 1-33)
  ○ Priscilla is an important Teacher. (Acts 18; Romans 16)
  ○ Jonathan reminds us of loyalty to a friend. (1 Samuel 13)
  ○ Orphans and Widows: serving those who need us most. (James 1.27)

• Some are examples of people who teach us about the consequences of poor choices:
  ○ Jezebel (1 Kings)
  ○ Herod (Matthew 2)
  ○ Goliath (1Samuel 17)
  ○ Eve (Genesis 3)
  ○ Zechariah (Luke 1)

• These are, in their essence, rhymes that teach all of us, adults as well as children, the wisdom of following Jesus' Greatest Commandment:

" 'Love the Lord your God with all your heart and with all your soul and with all your mind... and Love your neighbor as yourself.' This is the first and greatest commandment."
(Matthew 22.37,38)

Suggestions on How to Use this Book
and the
Alphabet Bible Characters Three Volume Set

Get a box big enough to hold a large number of small, inexpensive prizes. The prizes can be donated from a wish list if you are using these books in a classroom setting. Decorate the box and label it King Solomon's Treasure Chest. The child or children who can accomplish one of the following learning tasks are invited to take from the treasure chest one prize of their choosing per class period. The more difficult tasks are for the older children and the easier tasks are for the younger members of your group. To find a treasure chest to purchase, try Google or your favorite search engine and type the words "treasure chest prop." You'll find several choices.

More difficult tasks

1. Memorize and recite for the class one of the simple 4-line poems about a chosen character from the Alphabet Bible Characters books.
2. Identify the Book(s) of the Bible in which the Character appears and tell if it is Old or New Testament.
3. Tell what the character's symbol is for three different characters.
4. Name three characters and tell if each of the characters is in the Old or New Testament.
5. Name in alphabetical order seven characters in a row.
6. Get all of the five Quiz questions right about three different characters.
7. Memorize the Bible verse about the character- Two prizes
8. Three symbols games on pages 86 - 88; draw a line from the character's name in the list to the symbol of that character. 8 correct answers = One prize; 16 correct answers = Two prizes; All correct answers = Four prizes. (This page can be copied several times so the student can have another chance at guessing in a future class period.)

Easier Tasks

1. Color the entire character or characters on a page.
2. Identify the character by name and tell the class why you like this character.
3. Color the Symbols of four different characters. (Can be done in 4 successive class periods)
4. Save all the pages in a folder in alphabetical order for 3 prizes. (Can be done for each of the three alphabetical divisions of this book; 26 pages each.)
5. Name three characters that end with the same letter.

Published by Peeler-Rose Media
a division of Peeler-Rose Productions LLC

For information regarding permission
write to:
Peeler-Rose Productions LLC
ATTN: Permissions Department
8626 Aldwick Drive
Dallas, Texas 75238

Library of Congress Cataloging-in-Publication Data Peeler, Daniel; Rose Charles
Alphabet Bible Quiz And Color (Quiz 'N Color) Pages
Teacher's Edition
by Dan Peeler, Charlie Rose

Summary:
This volume contains a compiled book of lessons in the form of a coloring sheet and short quiz which
accompanies the previously published Alphabet Bible Character series Volumes 1 - 3. Each page is a
teacher's master intended for copying for Sunday School and Children's church activities.
Scripture reference is included.

Alphabetical Table of Contents

There was a Prophet named Jonah who God saved from drowning by sending a Great Fish to swallow him and deposit him on the shore of Nineveh. He was instructed by God to speak the word of truth to this city of Israel's enemies. Jonah said, "40 more days and Nineveh will be overturned." Sure enough, this city of Jonah's enemies believed in God's love for their people 40 days later. -Excerpt from Jonah 3. 1-10

A is for Anna

There was also a prophet, Anna the daughter of Phanuel, of the tribe of Asher... She never left the temple but worshipped there with fasting and prayer night and day.

Luke 2. 36-37 (NRSV)

Quiz - (see answers in back)

1. Anna lives in Chapter _____ of the Book of _____ .

2. Anna spent a lot of time _____ (gtsfian).

3. She was a _____ (rotpphe)

4. She met Mary and _____ with their baby.

5. The _____ is where Anna the Prophet prayed for many years.

B is for Barnabas

But Barnabas took him, brought him to the apostles, and described for them how on the road he had seen the Lord, who had spoken to him...

Acts 9. 27 (NRSV)

Quiz - (see answers in back)

1. Barnabas was a friend of _____ .

2. Barnabas told the other apostles that Paul had seen the _____on the road.

3. Paul was also an _____(psoalet).

4. Barnabas_____(akledw) for many miles to tell people about_____(sjseu).

5. Many pairs of these shoes called_____would have been worn out by Barnabas.

C is for Cornelius

In Caesarea there was a man named Cornelius, a centurion of the Italian Cohort, as it was called. He was a devout man who feared God with all his household; he gave alms generously to the people and prayed constantly to God.

Acts 10. 1-2 (NRSV)

Quiz - (see answers in back)

1. Cornelius was a _____.

2. He lived in a town called _____.

3. He gave alms (money) to the people and was very_____(ergeosun).

4. Cornelius and his whole _____ prayed to God.

5. A _____ was worn by Cornelius and by all Roman Centurions

D is for Deborah

At that time Deborah, a prophet, wife of Lappidoth, was judging Israel. She used to sit under the palm of Deborah between Ramah and Bethel in the hill country of Ephraim; and the Israelites came up to her for judgment.

Judges 4. 4-5 (NRSV)

Quiz - (See answers in back)

1. Deborah was a _____(uegjd) of Israel.

2. She did her work outdoors, sitting under a _____ tree, where people came for help.

3. Deborah's husband was named _____ .

4. The hill country was where the tribe of _____ (hpemair) lived.

5. The _____ is Deborah's symbol.

E is for Elizabeth

[Zechariah's] wife was a descendant of Aaron, and her name was Elizabeth. Both of them were righteous before God, living blamelessly according to all the commandments and regulations of the Lord.

Luke 1. 5-6 (NRSV)

Quiz - (See answers in back)

1. Elizabeth was a good woman who lived
_____(eellyabesms).

2. She was the mother of:
a. Peter b. Andrew c. Lydia   d. John the Baptist

3. One of Elizabeth's early relatives was the Priest, Aaron, the brother of (somes) _____ and (ammrii) _____ .

4. Elizabeth lives in the first chapter of the gospel of_____.

5. The sea_____of Baptism reminds us of Elizabeth.

F is for Fishers

And Jesus said to them, 'Follow me and I will make you fish for people.' And immediately they left their nets and followed him.

Mark 1. 17-18 (NRSV)

Quiz - (See answers in back)

1. Peter, Andrew, James, and _____ were four of Jesus' early followers.

2. For a living, they caught _____ (ihsf) in their _____ (tens)

3. They spent the rest of their lives fishing for_____ .

4. Jesus told them _____ _____ (loofwl em).

5. The _____ reminds us of these four fishers of people.

G is for Gideon

[Gideon] put trumpets into the hands of all of them, and empty jars, with torches inside the jars; he said to them, 'Look at me, and do the same; when I come to the outskirts of the camp, do as I do.'

Judges 7. 16-17 (NRSV)

Quiz - (See answers in back)

1. Gideon's soldiers carried _____ (rasj), _____ (crothse) and _____ (pmuretts).

2. Gideons story is in the Book of _____.

3. He followed God's commands even though he did not _____ (suedrtnadn) all of them.

4. Gideon said, " _____ (okol) at me and do the _____ " (mase).

5. Gideon's _____ was made out of a ram's horn.

H is for Huldah

So the priests ... went to the prophet Huldah...she resided in Jerusalem in the Second Quarter, where they consulted her.

2 Kings 22. 14 (NRSV)

Quiz - (See answers in back)

1. Huldah was a wise woman who was _____ (lusnotcde) by many people.

2. The part of Jerusalem where Huldah lived was called the _____ (cesnod) _____ (urtqare).

3. In this story, she is visited by _____ .

4. Huldah lives in the Book of _____.

5. The _____ were taken to Huldah for answers.

I is for Isaiah

[God said to Isaiah] The wolf shall live with the lamb, the leopard shall lie down with the kid, the calf and the lion and the fatling together, and a little child shall lead them.

Isaiah 11.6 (NRSV)

Quiz - (See answers in back)

1. Isaiah was a prophet who was given special knowledge from _____ (oGd).

2. Isaiah could see a time when there was no war and _____ (lvsewo) lived with _____(blmas).

3. He said people would learn how to be peaceful from:
a) soldiers b) kings c) a child d) turkeys .

4. Isaiah's story is in the Book of _____ .

5. The _____ and the _____ are the symbols of Isaiah.

J is for Joanna

...Mary, called Magdalene...and Joanna, the wife of Herod's steward Chuza, and Susanna, and many others, who provided for them out of their resources.

Luke 8. 3 (NRSV)

Quiz - (See answers in back)

1. Joanna is listed among several people who _____ (ropdevid) money to help Jesus travel.

2. Joanna's husband worked in the court of:
a. Solomon b. Saul c. Herod d. Jonathan

3. Joanna's friends were _____ (rmya ladageenm) and _____ (nasansu).

4. The Gospel writer _____, tells the story of Joanna.

5. The open _____ reminds us of the generous Joanna.

K is for King David

[David] took his staff in his hand, and chose five smooth stones from the wadi, and put them in his shepherd's bag, in the pouch; his sling was in his hand, and he drew near to the Philistine.

1 Samuel 17.40 (NRSV)

Quiz - (See answers in back)

1. When David was young he was a _____(hehpsdre).

2. In order to protect his sheep from wild animals, David flung

_____(notess) from a _____(nilgs).

3. Young David stood up to the Philistine Warrior named:

a. Hercules   b. Samson   c. Goliath   d. Bob

4. We first meet David in the Book of_____.

5. The _____ reminds that David was a great king.

L is for Lydia

A certain woman named Lydia, a worshipper of God, was listening to us; she was from the city of Thyatira and a dealer in purple cloth.

Acts 16.14 (NRSV)

Quiz - (See answers in back)

1. Lydia sold expensive fabric that was:

a. pink   b. purple   c. plaid   d. polyester

2. When Lydia met Paul, she was already

a_____(rewsowhpip) of God.

3. Lydia's story is in the Book of _____.

4. Paul taught Lydia about Christ in _____(tayrihat)

5. A bolt of _____reminds us of Lydia.

M is for Miriam

Then the prophet Miriam, Aaron's sister, took a tambourine in her hand; and all the women went out after her with tambourines and with dancing.

Exodus 15.20 (NRSV)

Quiz - (See answers in back)

1. Miriam was a _____(porteph) who was the older sister of

Aaron and _____(esmso).

2. Miriam liked to celebrate with;

a. Chips and dips   b. malted shakes   c. music   d. long walks

3. She watched over her baby brother in the Book of _____.

4. Miriam liked to make music:

a. alone   b. on a stage   c. with other people

5. The _____is the instrument Miriam played.

N is for Nicodemus

Now there was a Pharisee named Nicodemus, a leader of the Jews. He came to Jesus* by night and said to him, 'Rabbi, we know that you are a teacher who has come from God; for no one can do these signs that you do apart from the presence of God.'

John 3. 1-2 (NRSV)

Quiz - (See answers in back)

1. Nicodemus was a _____(siehaper).

2. He believed that Jesus had come from_____.

3. Nicodemus talked to Jesus in:

a. The afternoon   b. the living room   c. the dark of night

4. A Rabbi is a:

a. Carpenter   b. Teacher   c. Long-eared animal

5. The _____reminds us of Nicodemus' night visit.

O is for Onesimus

I am appealing to you for my child, Onesimus, whose father I have become during my imprisonment.

Philemon 1. 10 (NRSV)

Quiz - (See answers in back)

1. Onesimus was a runaway slave who met the Apostle Paul

in _____. (ripnos)

2. Paul wrote a letter praising the kindness of Onesimus to his

master, _____(milehopn).

3. Paul felt as if Onesimus was his _____ and that he was

Onesimus' _____.

4. Paul was being held in prison for:

a. fighting with Peter   b. traffic tickets   c. preaching

5. Sometimes bracelets were worn by _____ like Onesimus.

P is for Phoebe

I commend to you our sister Phoebe, a deacon of the church at Cenchreae, so that you may welcome her in the Lord as is fitting for the saints, and help her in whatever she may require from you, for she has been a benefactor of many and of myself as well.

Romans 16.1-2 (NRSV)

Quiz - (See answers in back)

1. Phoebe was a _____ of the church.

2. She was an important leader who preached, taught and served

in a town called_____(cheneaerc).

3. She took Paul's letter to the Romans, who Paul asked to

_____(lewmoce) her and help her.

4. Phoebe is commended in the letter to the

_____(marnos).

5. The _____letter is the symbol of Phoebe.

Q is for Queen of Sheba

When the Queen of Sheba heard of the fame of Solomon, (fame due to the name of the Lord), she came to test him with hard questions.

1 Kings 10. 1-13 (NRSV)

Quiz - (See answers in back)

1. The Queen of Sheba was an important ruler who visited

King_____(nomolso).

2. Solomon was wise because he prayed for wisdom from

_____(the rodL).

3. The Queen of Sheba came to test him with:

a. An art contest b. hard questions c. a tennis match

4. Sheba's story is found in the book of _____.

5. A crown topped with_____ reminds us of the Queen of Sheba.

R is for Ruth

But Ruth said, 'Do not press me to leave you or to turn back from following you! Where you go, I will go; where you lodge, I will lodge; your people shall be my people, and your God my God.

Ruth 1. 16 (NRSV)

Quiz - (See answers in back)

1. Ruth told Naomi not to ask her to turn back from _____(llofwongi).

2. She said that "your _____(opepel) will be my_____ (ppeelo) and your (doG)_____my_____(odG)".

3. When Ruth tells Naomi they will share the same "lodge," she means:

a. the state park   b. the same home   c. a treehouse

4. Ruth and Naomi's story is in the Book of _____.

5. The _____was gathered by Ruth to help Naomi.

S is for Samuel

...Samuel was lying down in the temple of the Lord, where the ark of God was. Then the Lord called, 'Samuel! Samuel!'* and he said, 'Here I am!'

1 Samuel 3. 3-4 (NRSV)

Quiz - (See answers in back)

1. When the Prophet Samuel was a young boy, he lived, worked

and slept in the_____(etmlep).

2. As Samuel was sleeping one evening, he heard:

 a. A dog barking   b. hammering   c. the voice of God.

3. When Samuel heard the voice, he said:

 a. Who are you?   b. I'm trying to sleep.   c. Here I am.

4. This story is found in the Book of _____.

5. A new _____was brought to Samuel by his mother, Hannah.

T is for Tabitha

Now in Joppa there was a disciple whose name was Tabitha, which in Greek is Dorcas.* She was devoted to good works and acts of charity.

Acts 9. 36 (NRSV)

Quiz - (See answers in back)

1. In Joppa, a seacoast town near Jerusalem, a woman named

Tabitha lived as a _____ (sildepic) of Jesus.

2. Tabitha was well known in the town for her:

 a. singing ability   b. acts of charity   c. fishing boat

3. Tabitha was also known as Dorcas, meaning "deer" in the

_____ (eekrg) language.

4. Tabitha lives in the Book of _____.

5. Tabitha used a _____ and thread to sew clothing for those in need.

U is for Uriah

In the letter [King David] wrote, 'Set Uriah in the forefront of the hardest fighting...
2 Samuel 11. 15 (NRSV)

Quiz - (See answers in back)

1. Uriah was a loyal soldier in the army of King:

 a. Saul   b. Henry   c. David

2. Uriah was married to Bathsheba, who King David also wanted

as his: a. dance partner   b. wife   c. governor

3. Sadly, David wanted to get rid of Uriah, and put him in the

_____ (oroteffrn) of _____(ithfgign).

4. This story of David and Uriah is in the Book of

_____.

5. The dented_____ reminds us of Uriah.

25

V is for Visitors

In the time of King Herod, after Jesus was born in Bethlehem of Judea, magi from the East came to Jerusalem, asking, 'Where is the child who has been born king of the Jews?

Matthew 2. 1-2 (NRSV)

Quiz - (See answers in back)

1. The visitors to the baby Jesus were called

_____ from the east.

2. They came to Herod's palace to ask him "Where is the

_____ who has been born king of the _____

(wsej)?"

3. Jesus had been born in:

  a. Jerusalem b. Bethlehem c. Kansas

4. The visitors from the east are found in the Gospel of

_____ .

5. The three _____ were brought by the visitors called magi.

W is for Widow

Now the wife of a member of the company of prophets cried to Elisha, 'Your servant my husband is dead; and you know that your servant feared the Lord, but a creditor has come to take my two children as slaves.'

2 Kings 4. 1 (NRSV)

Quiz - (See answers in back)

1. The Widow told her sad story to the Prophet _____.

2. In these long ago days, to pay off a debt, people sometimes sent

their own children to be:

 a. soldiers   b. puppeteers   c. slaves

3. The Widow's husband had also been a

_____ (rpeopth).

4. Her story is in the Book of _____.

5. The _____ reminds us of the containers of oil.

X is for Xerxes

...the king [Xerxes] again said to Esther, 'What is your petition, Queen Esther? It shall be granted you. And what is your request? Even to the half of my kingdom, it shall be fulfilled.'

Esther 7. 2 (NRSV)

Quiz - (See answers in back)

1. King Ahasuerus of Persia was also called _____

(eexxsr).

2. His wife the queen was named Esther and her people were the:

  a. Egyptians   b. Jews   c. Philadelphians

3. Xerxes offered Esther half of his:

  a. allowance   b. sandwich   c. kingdom

4. Xerxes is found in the Book of_____.

5. The _____is the type of crown Xerxes wore.

Y is for Yahweh

The Lord is my light and my salvation; whom shall I fear?

Psalm 27.1 (NRSV)

Quiz - (See answers in back)

1. The name, Yahweh, was never spoken by the Hebrew people because they believed it was too:

a. hard to remember   b. holy to be spoken   c. hard to pronounce

2. When God's name was to be written down, sometimes the Bible writers would use other words in its place, such as:

a. The Person Upstairs   b. The Force   c. The Lord

3. Some form of God's name or a mention of God is in every Book of the Bible except:

a. Exodus   b. Esther   c. Ruth

4. The One God of the Hebrew People was called_____(heyhaw).

5. The _____ reminds us of Yahweh.

29

Z is for Zipporah

Moses agreed to stay with the man, and he gave Moses his daughter Zipporah in marriage.
Exodus 2.21 (NRSV)

Quiz - (See answers in back)

1. Moses drove away bullies from Jethro's daughters at a well. One of

the daughters was named _____(hapropzi).

2. Zipporah was from the land of :

  a. Israel   b. Midian   c. Australia

3. Zipporah once performed a religious duty and saved Moses':

  a. cloak   b. staff c. life

4. In Zipporah's time, fathers could give their daughters to another

man in _____(rarmigae)

5. The _____ of the Law remind us of Zipporah.

A is for Abraham

Now the Lord said to Abram, 'Go from your country and your kindred and your father's house to the land that I will show you. I will make of you a great nation, and I will bless you, and make your name great, so that you will be a blessing.

Genesis 12.1-2

Quiz - (See answers in back)

1. Abraham was first called _____(maarb).

2. God told Abraham to leave his land and his father's

_____.

3. God promised that Abraham's family would be a great

_____ that would be a _____(lbensigs) to many.

4. God first speaks to Abraham in the Book of _____.

5. The staff of a _____ reminds us of Abraham.

B is for Bathsheba

[Bathsheba] said to him, 'My lord, you swore to your servant by the Lord your God, saying: Your son Solomon shall succeed me as king, and he shall sit on my throne.

1 Kings 1.17

Quiz - (See answers in back)

1. King David and _____(abethhsab) were the parents

of _____(ooomlsn).

2. Bathsheba wanted her son to be the next _____.

3. She reminded David that he had said Solomon would sit on his

_____(northe).

4. This story of Bathsheba is in the first chapter of

_____.

5. The Queen's _____
reminds us of Bathsheba.

C is for Caleb

But my servant Caleb, because he has a different spirit and has followed me wholeheartedly, I will bring into the land into which he went, and his descendants shall possess it.

Numbers 14.24

Quiz - (See answers in back)

1. God was pleased with Caleb's _____(riptsi).

2. Caleb had followed

God_____(ratholewhyelde).

3. God said that Caleb's children and grandchildren and their

grandchildren would possess the_____.

4. Caleb's story counts because it is in the Book of

_____.

5. Caleb had milk and _____ in the new land.

D is for Delilah

So Delilah said to Samson, 'Please tell me what makes your strength so great, and how you could be bound, so that one could subdue you.'

Judges 16.6

Quiz - (See answers in back)

1. Delilah wanted to know how Samson could be

_____(donub).

2. She wanted him to tell her the secret of his

great_____.

3. Samson became weak after Delilah got someone to cut his:

a. Lawn   b. Hair   c. Allowance

4. Delilah's story is in Chapter 16 of the Book of

_____.

5. _____remind us of Delilah.

E is for Elijah

As [Elijah and Elisha] continued walking and talking, a chariot of fire and horses of fire separated the two of them, and Elijah ascended in a whirlwind into heaven.

2 Kings 2.11

Quiz - (See answers in back)

1. The Prophets Elijah and Elisha were outside

_____and _____.

2. An amazing thing suddenly came between them. It was a

flaming:

a. Sword   b. Motorcycle   c. Chariot

3. Elijah flew away in a_____(rihniwdlw).

4. This story is in the second Book of _____.

5. The flaming _____is a symbol of Elijah

F is for Flood Family

And Noah with his sons and his wife and his sons' wives went into the ark to escape the waters of the flood.

Genesis 7.7

Quiz - (See answers in back)

1. Noah and his wife had three sons. How many people were on the ark?

a. 5   b. 12   c. 8

2. They went into the ark to escape the_____ of the

_____ .

3. The ark also was filled with a lot of:

a. Deck chairs   b. board games   c. animals

4. _____ (neegiss) is the Book that tells about the flood.

5. The _____ reminds us of God's promise after the flood.

G is for Gabriel

The angel [Gabriel] said to her, 'Do not be afraid, Mary, for you have found favor with God. And now, you will conceive in your womb and bear a son, and you will name him Jesus.

Luke 1.30,31

Quiz - (See answers in back)

1. Gabriel told Mary not to be _____.

2. Gabriel said Mary would name her son:

a. Joseph   b. Bob   c. Jesus

3. Angels are God's _____ (esesmegnrs).

4. The Gospel of _____ tells about the visit of Gabriel.

5. This _____ with a message scroll is Gabriel.

H is for Hagar

And God heard the voice of the boy; and the angel of God called to Hagar from heaven, and said to her, 'What troubles you, Hagar? Do not be afraid; for God has heard the voice of the boy where he is. Come, lift up the boy and hold him fast with your hand, for I will make a great nation of him.'

Genesis 21. 17-18

Quiz - (See answers in back)

1. Hagar's son Ishmael was thirsty in the desert, but God heard the _____ of the boy.

2. Hagar was told her son would be part of a _____ (terga) _____ (tonina).

3. Hagar, an Egyptian slave girl, heard a voice from:

a. Heaven   b. Kansas   c. inside herself

4. The Book of _____ tells Hagar's story.

5. The Egyptian _____ reminds us of Hagar.

38

I is for Israel

Now Israel loved Joseph more than any other of his children, because he was the son of his old age; and he had made him a long robe with sleeves. [a coat of many colors]

Genesis 37.3

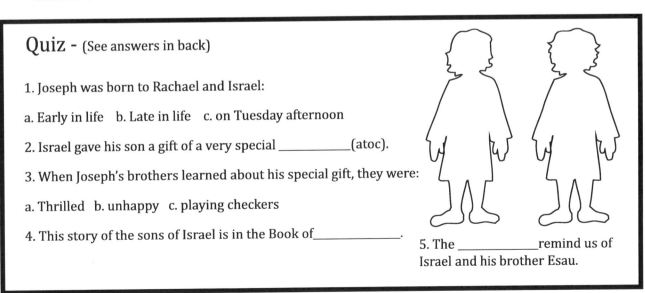

Quiz - (See answers in back)

1. Joseph was born to Rachael and Israel:

a. Early in life   b. Late in life   c. on Tuesday afternoon

2. Israel gave his son a gift of a very special _____(atoc).

3. When Joseph's brothers learned about his special gift, they were:

a. Thrilled   b. unhappy   c. playing checkers

4. This story of the sons of Israel is in the Book of_____.

5. The _____ remind us of Israel and his brother Esau.

J is for Jochebed

When [Jochebed] could hide him no longer, she got a papyrus basket for him and plastered it with bitumen and pitch; she put the child in it and placed it among the reeds on the bank of the river.

Exodus 2.3

Quiz - (See answers in back)

1. Jochebed hid her baby son, Moses, in a basket made of

_____ (yapuprs).

2. So that it would not sink, she sealed the basket with

_____ and _____.

3. Jochebed hid her baby son from the soldiers of the:

a. Pharaoh   b. Philistines   c. Canadians

4. We can find Jochebed in the book of _____ .

5. The floating _____ was made by Jochebed.

K is for King Darius

Then, at break of day, [King Darius] got up and hurried to the den of lions. When he came near the den where Daniel was, he cried out anxiously to Daniel, 'O Daniel, servant of the living God, has your God whom you faithfully serve been able to deliver you from the lions?'

Daniel 6.19-20

Quiz - (See answers in back)

1. King Darius hurried to the den of lions in:

a. The afternoon   b. the early morning   c. his pajamas

2. Darius hoped Daniel would be protected by the

_____God whom Daniel faithfully served.

3. Darius asked Daniel if he had been

_____(veelridde) from the (nolsi).

4. The story of Daniel and King Darius is in the Book of

_____.

5. The _____of Babylon is the symbol of Darius.

41

L is for Lois

I am reminded of your sincere faith, a faith that lived first in your grandmother Lois and your mother Eunice and now, I am sure, lives in you.

2 Timothy 1.5

Quiz - (See answers in back)

1. The Apostle Paul wrote about Lois who was Timothy's

_____.

2. Timothy's mother was named _____(cieuen).

3. Timothy was taught by his grandmother about:

a. Cooking   b. chariot repair   c. faith

4. We learn about Lois in Paul's second letter to

_____.

5. The chalk and _____remind us of Lois.

M is for Martha

But Martha was distracted by her many tasks; so she came to him and asked, 'Lord, do you not care that my sister has left me to do all the work by myself? Tell her then to help me.' But the Lord answered her, 'Martha, Martha, you are worried and distracted by many things;

Luke 10.40-41

Quiz - (See answers in back)

1. Martha was _____(tacderistd) by her many

tasks.

2. Martha wanted Jesus to tell her _____to help

Martha with her _____.

3. Jesus didn't want Martha to_____(rowry) so

much.

4. This version of Martha's story is in:

a. Exodus b. a hurry c. Luke

5. The _____is busy Martha's symbol.

N is for Naomi

[Obed] shall be to you a restorer of life and a nourisher of your old age; for your daughter-in-law who loves you, who is more to you than seven sons, has borne him.'

Ruth 4. 14-15

Quiz - (See answers in back)

1. Naomi was told that her new grandson, Obed, would be a
_____(tesrorre) of life.

2. Naomi had known much sadness in her life, but her
daughter-in-law meant more to her than
_____(veens)_____(noss).

3. Naomi's daughter-in-law was named:
a. Harriet   b. Jochebed   c. Ruth

4. Naomi's story is in the Book of _____.

5. A new _____reminds us of Naomi's new life.

44

O is for Obadiah

Though you soar aloft like the eagle, though your nest is set among the stars, from there I will bring you down, says the Lord.

Obadiah 1.4

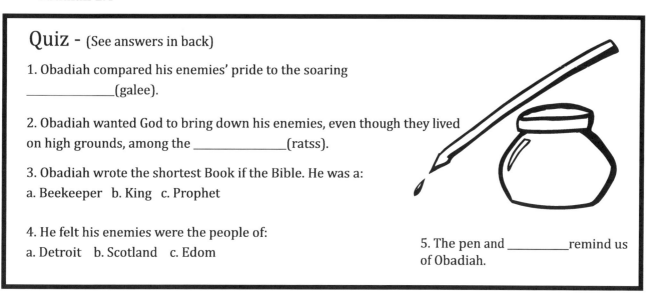

Quiz - (See answers in back)

1. Obadiah compared his enemies' pride to the soaring _____(galee).

2. Obadiah wanted God to bring down his enemies, even though they lived on high grounds, among the _____(ratss).

3. Obadiah wrote the shortest Book if the Bible. He was a:
a. Beekeeper   b. King   c. Prophet

4. He felt his enemies were the people of:
a. Detroit   b. Scotland   c. Edom

5. The pen and _____remind us of Obadiah.

P is for Priscilla

He [Apollos] began to speak boldly in the synagogue; but when Priscilla and Aquila heard him, they took him aside and explained the Way of God to him more accurately.

Acts 18.26

Quiz - (See answers in back)

1. Priscilla was a friend of the Apostle Paul. She explained the _____ of _____ to the preacher, Apollos.

2. Priscilla's husband was named _____(qauali).

3. Priscilla, Aquila and Paul taught people about Jesus. They were also: a. Folksingers   b. tentmakers   c. puppeteers

4. Priscilla is mentioned in Paul's letters and also in the Book of: a. Genesis   b. Hiking   c. Acts

5. The welcoming _____is Priscilla's symbol.

Q is for Qohelet

For everything there is a season, and a time for every matter under heaven: a time to be born, and a time to die; a time to plant, and a time to pluck up what is planted . . .

Ecclesiastes 3.1-2

Quiz - (See answers in back)

1. "Qohelet" means teacher or preacher. He said that for everything, there is a _____ (eassno).

2. Qohelet said that everyone is the same because every person has a time to be _____ and a time to_____.

3. He said that if we plant something, we must also:
a. Prune it   b. pluck it   c. paint it red

4. Qohelet's sayings are in the Book of _____.

5. Qohelet's symbol is the autumn _____.

R is for Rahab

Then the king of Jericho sent orders to Rahab, 'Bring out the men who have come to you, who entered your house, for they have come only to search out the whole land.' But the woman took the two men and hid them.

Joshua 2. 3-4

Quiz - (See answers in back)

1. Rahab lived in Jericho where she hid two Hebrew visitors

from the_____ of Jericho.

2. The men were in her _____ (euosh).

3. The men had come to search out the:

a. Laundromat   b. land   c. theme park

4. Rahab's story is in the Book of _____.

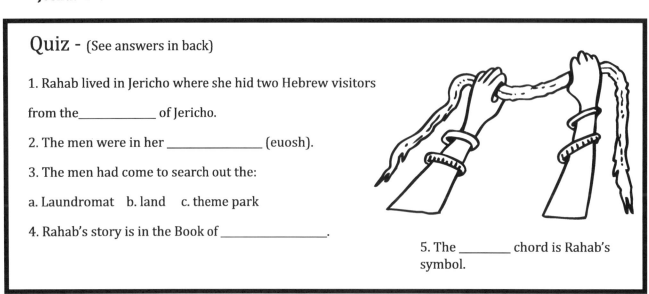

5. The _____ chord is Rahab's symbol.

S is for Sarah

Then one said, 'I will surely return to you in due season, and your wife Sarah shall have a son.' So Sarah laughed to herself, saying, 'After I have grown old, and my husband is old, shall I have pleasure?'

Genesis 18. 10, 12

Quiz - (See answers in back)

1. When Sarah heard three visitors tell her husband Abraham that she would have a baby, she _____ to herself.

2. She didn't think she could have a baby because she was too:

a. Busy   b. far south   c. old

3. Having a son was too good to believe. She never thought she would have that _____ (seaulper).

4. Sarah laughs in the Book of _____.

5. The _____ are Sarah's symbols of many children.

T is for Thomas

Then [Jesus] said to Thomas, 'Put your finger here and see my hands. Reach out your hand and put it in my side. Do not doubt but believe.' Thomas answered him, 'My Lord and my God!

John 20. 27-28

Quiz - (See answers in back)

1. Thomas questioned what the other people said about

_____(ussej) rising again.

2. Jesus said to Thomas, "Do not _____, but believe."

3. Thomas called Jesus, "My _____and my_____.

4. Thomas was one of Jesus':

a. Tailors   b. personal trainers   c. disciples

5. An architect's _____ is on the shield of Thomas.

U is for Uzziah

But when he had become strong he grew proud, to his destruction. For he was false to the Lord his God, and entered the temple of the Lord to make offering on the altar of incense.

2 Chronicles 26.16

Quiz - (See answers in back)

1. Uzziah was a king who became too _____

(ourdp).

2. He thought he could do the job of a priest and make an

_____ in the Temple.

3. God's law allowed only priests to make offerings, so Uzziah

was _____ to the Lord his God.

4. Uzziah's story is in the Book of:

a. Really Bad Kings   b. Genesis   c. 2 Chronicles

5. Uzziah's symbol is the
_____ scepter.

V is for Vashti

... the king...commanded [them] to bring Queen Vashti before the king, wearing the royal crown, in order to show the peoples and the officials her beauty; for she was fair to behold. But Queen Vashti refused to come at the king's command...

Esther 1.10-12

Quiz - (See answers in back)

1.   The King sent his servants to Queen Vashti to tell her

to display her: a.   Model cars   b. beauty   c. goldfish

2.   Queen Vashti refused to follow the king's

_____.

3.   She would not even wear her royal

_____(rwocn).

4.   Vashti's brave act is in the Book of _____.

5. The discarded _____ is Queen Vashti's symbol.

52

W is for Woman Wisdom

Happy are those who find wisdom, and those who get understanding, for her income is better than silver, and her revenue better than gold.

Proverbs 3. 13-14

Quiz - (See answers in back)

1. The writer of Proverbs used the symbol of a woman for

_____ (sidmow).

2. Woman Wisdom's knowledge and understanding are

better than _____(vislre) and _____(lodg).

3. Those who find her are:
a. Tired   b. Happy   c. Zookeepers

4. Wisdom is seen as a woman in _____.

5. Precious _____ remind us of Woman Wisdom.

X is for Andrew's Cross

One of the two who heard John speak and followed Jesus was Andrew, Simon Peter's brother.

John 1. 40

Quiz - (See answers in back)

1. Andrew was listening to what _____the Baptist said and

decided to follow_____.

2. Andrew's brother was:

a. Moses   b. Barnabas   c. Simon Peter

3. Some people think that after preaching for many years,

Andrew died on a _____ (rscos) shaped like an "X."

4. Andrew is mentioned in all four _____(sogslep).

5. Andrew's symbol is the "X" shaped _____.

Y is for Young Jesus

After three days they found him in the temple, sitting among the teachers, listening to them and asking them questions. And all who heard him were amazed at his understanding and his answers.

Luke 2.46-47

Quiz - (See answers in back)

1. Once Mary and Joseph lost their young son, _____ in the city of Jerusalem.

2. They looked and looked for their son for:
a. Two hours   b. three days   c. four years

3. They found him in the _____ amazing all the wise _____ with his understanding of God's word.

4. Young Jesus' parents looked for him in the Gospel of_____.

5. The _____ of the Temple is where Jesus talked to the teachers.

Z is for Zacchaeus

When Jesus came to the place, he looked up and said to him, 'Zacchaeus, hurry and come down; for I must stay at your house today.' So he hurried down and was happy to welcome him.

Luke 19. 5-6

Quiz - (See answers in back)

1. Zacchaeus climbed up in a Sycamore tree to get a look

at_____(sejus).

2. Jesus said, "I must _____at your _____ today."

3. After he heard what Jesus said, Zacchaeus:

a. Fell on his head   b. climbed higher   c. hurried down

4. Zacchaeus' story is in the Gospel of_____.

5. The Sycamore _____was climbed by Zacchaeus.

A is for Abigail

Then Abigail hurried and took two hundred loaves, two skins of wine, five sheep ready dressed, five measures of parched grain, one hundred clusters of raisins, and two hundred cakes of figs. She loaded them on donkeys and said to her young men, 'Go on ahead of me; I am coming after you.'

1 Samuel 25. 18-19

Quiz - (See answers in back)

1. Abigail took a lot of food to David and his small army, including two _____ cakes of figs.

2. She had the young men who worked for her take the food to David on _____ (nokyesd).

3. Abigail sent the men ahead of her, but said, "I am:
a. coming after you.   b. on a diet.   c. in need of more donkeys.

4. Abigail's story is in the first Book of _____.

5. A plate of _____ is Abigail's symbol.

B is for Bezalel

The Lord spoke to Moses: See, I have called by name Bezalel son of Uri, son of Hur, of the tribe of Judah: and I have filled him with divine spirit,* with ability, intelligence, and knowledge in every kind of craft, to devise artistic designs, to work in gold, silver, and bronze, in cutting stones for setting, and in carving wood, in every kind of craft.

Exodus 31.1- 5

Quiz - (See answers in back)

1. Moses needed someone to build the Tabernacle. God sent him a man named_____.

2. Bezalel was a gifted artist who had been filled with _____(vinide) _____(riptis).

3. To build the Ark of the Covenant, Bezalel would have worked in: a. Plastic   b. aluminum foil   c. Gold and wood

4. Bezalel builds all the holy objects in the Book of_____.

5. The Menorah was also built by_____.

C is for Centurion

When [Jesus] entered Capernaum, a centurion came to him, appealing to him and saying, 'Lord, my servant is lying at home paralyzed, in terrible distress.' And he said to him, 'I will come and cure him.' The centurion answered, 'Lord, I am not worthy to have you come under my roof; but only speak the word, and my servant will be healed.

Matthew 8. 5-8

Quiz - (See answers in back)

1. The Roman soldier, the centurion, was upset because his servant

was _____(zapardely).

2. Jesus offered to:

a. Call a doctor   b. come and cure him   c. send help

3. The humble centurion said he was not worthy to have Jesus

come under his _____.

4. The Gospel of _____tells this story.

5. The breastplate of faith was worn by the _____.

D is for Dinah

Now Dinah the daughter of Leah, whom she had borne to Jacob, went out to visit the women of the region.

Genesis 34.1

Quiz - (See answers in back)

1. Dinah was the daughter of _____ and _____.

2. Dinah went into the region to visit

the_____ (mowne).

3. Jacob wanted his daughter Dinah to marry the prince of the

region who was named: a. Burt   b. Ernie   c. Shechem

4. Dinah's story is in the Book of _____.

5. A torn veil is _____ symbol.

E is for Eve

The woman said to the serpent, 'We may eat of the fruit of the trees in the garden; but God said, "You shall not eat of the fruit of the tree that is in the middle of the garden, nor shall you touch it, or you shall die." '

Genesis 3.2

Quiz - (See answers in back)

1. Eve talked to a:

a. Dinosaur   b. vampire bat   c. snake

2. She said God had told Eve and Adam not to eat from the tree

in the _____(dimdel) of the garden.

3. God had said that if they were to _____(tea) of the fruit or

even _____(couht) it, they would _____ (ide).

4. Eve's story is in the Book of _____.

5. The _____is the symbol of Eve.

F is for Four Daughters

[Philip the evangelist] had four unmarried daughters* who had the gift of prophecy.
Acts 21.9

Quiz - (See answers in back)

1. Paul's friend Philip was an _____(gavenislet).

2. He had four daughters who were not:

a. Home very often   b. blond   c. married

3. The four had the gift of _____(ropcepyh).

4. The four daughters are in the Book of _____.

5. The daughters' _____point up to God.

G is for Goliath

And [Goliath] the Philistine said, 'Today I defy the ranks of Israel! Give me a man, that we may fight together.'

1 Samuel 17.10

Quiz - (See answers in back)

1. Goliath was a soldier in the _____ (sitnepistlh) army.

2. He thought the army of Israel was cowardly and asked for just one man to:
a. Give him directions   b. fight   c. bring him lunch

3. Goliath said, "Today I _____ the army, or ranks, of Israel."

4. Goliath fights David in the Book of _____.

5. David's _____ and sling remind us of Goliath.

H is for Hannah

Hannah prayed and said, 'My heart exults in the Lord; my strength is exalted in my God.

1 Samuel 2.1

Quiz - (See answers in back)

1. Faithful said her heart _____ in the Lord,

meaning: has great joy.

2. Her strength was _____ which means: lifted up.

3. Hannah said these things when she was:

a. At a party   b. Having lunch   c. Praying

4. Hannah was Samuel's mother. Her story is in the Book of

_____.

5. Hannah made her son Samuel a new

_____ every year.

I is for Ishmael

God was with [Ishmael], and he grew up; he lived in the wilderness, and became an expert with the bow. He lived in the wilderness of Paran; and his mother got a wife for him from the land of

Egypt. Genesis 21. 20-21

Quiz - (See answers in back)

1. Ishmael lived in the _____. (derwlissen)

2. His mother, Hagar, found him a wife in _____.

(gtegpy)

3. Ishmael was an expert with the:

a. Paint brush b. needle c. bow

4. Ishmael's story is found in the Book of _____.

5. The _____ and arrow remind us of Ishmael.

J is for Jonathan

When David had finished speaking to Saul, the soul of Jonathan was bound to the soul of David, and Jonathan loved him as his own soul.

1 Samuel 18.1

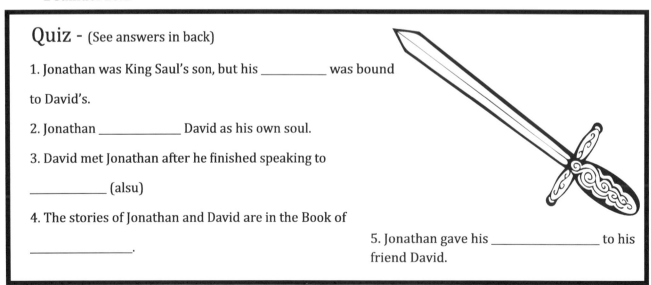

Quiz - (See answers in back)

1. Jonathan was King Saul's son, but his _____ was bound to David's.

2. Jonathan _____ David as his own soul.

3. David met Jonathan after he finished speaking to _____ (alsu)

4. The stories of Jonathan and David are in the Book of _____.

5. Jonathan gave his _____ to his friend David.

K is for King Herod

When King Herod heard this [news from the Magi] , he was frightened, and all Jerusalem with him; and calling together all the chief priests and scribes of the people, he inquired of them where the Messiah was to be born.

Matthew 2.3-4

Quiz - (See answers in back)

1. The Magi's news was about the birth of Jesus. Herod

was _____ (tengfrideh)

2. He called together the chief _____ and

_____.

3. Herod wanted to know where the _____ was

to be born.

4. We read about Herod in the Gospel of _____.

5. Like most Kings, Herod lived in a _____.

L is for Leah

Now Laban had two daughters; the name of the elder was Leah, and the name of the younger was Rachel. Leah's eyes were lovely,* and Rachel was graceful and beautiful.

Genesis 29.16-17

Quiz - (See answers in back)

1. Laban was Rebekah's brother.

How many daughters did he have?

a. seven   b. twenty-three   c. two

2. Leah's eyes were:

a. blue   b. squinted   c. lovely

3. Rachael was _____ and _____.

4. Jacob's two wives, Leah and Rachael, are in the Book of

5. Lovely _____ remind us of Leah.

M is for Mary Magdalene

After the Sabbath, as the first day of the week was dawning, Mary Magdalene and the other Mary went to see the tomb. And suddenly there was a great earthquake; for an angel of the Lord, descending from heaven, came and rolled back the stone and sat on it.

Matthew 28.1-2

Quiz - (See answers in back)

1. Mary Magdalene went to the empty tomb at:

a. Dinner time   b. dawn   c. noon

2. Suddenly there was a great _____

(aeathkequr)

3. An _____ of the Lord came down from

_____.

4. This story about Mary is in the Gospel of _____.

5. Mary took a jar of perfumed oil to the empty _____.

N is for Nehemiah

The words of Nehemiah son of Hacaliah: In the month of Chislev, in the twentieth year, while I was in Susa the capital, 2one of my brothers, Hanani, came with certain men from Judah; and I asked them about the Jews that survived, those who had escaped the captivity, and about Jerusalem.

Nehemiah 1.1-2

Quiz - (See answers in back)

1. Nehemiah heard news from his brother _____.

2. Nehemiah was worried about the people still living in:

a. Detroit   b. Babylon   c. Jerusalem

3. He asked about the _____ who had not been captured.

4. Nehemiah's story is in the Book of _____.

5. To mark where repairs were needed in Jerusalem, Nehemiah needed a _____.

O is for Orphans

Religion that is pure and undefiled before God ... is this: to care for orphans and widows in their distress, and to keep oneself unstained by the world.

James 1. 27

Quiz - (See answers in back)

1. James said that there is a _____ (erup)

religion before God.

2. He wrote we should help orphans and:

a. Rich people   b. widows   c. only people we like

3. People _____ by the world are not selfish.

4. This mention of orphans and widows is in the Book

(or letter) of _____.

5. Helping _____ remind us of serving the orphans.

P is for Puah

But the midwives [Shiphrah and Puah] feared God; they did not do as the king of Egypt commanded them, but they let the boys live.

Exodus 1.17

Quiz - (See answers in back)

1. Puah and Shiphrah were like nurses of long ago called _____.

2. The two women worshipped:

a. Deserts   b. God   c. Pharaoh

3. The king told them to kill the Hebrew baby boys, but they let the boys_____. (vile)

4. Shiphrah and Puah's story is in the Book of _____.

5. A _____ wrapped in a blanket reminds us of the two brave women.

72

Q is for Queen Jezebel

[Elijah said:] Now therefore send and gather all Israel to me at Mount Carmel, and the 450 prophets of Baal and the 400 prophets of Asherah, who eat at Jezebel's table."

1 Kings 18.19

Quiz - (See answers in back)

1. Jezebel worshipped two gods, named _____

(abla) and Asherah.

2. Elijah met how many prophets of the other gods on

Mount Carmel?   a. 19   b. 850   c. 500

3. The prophets were so important to Queen Jezebel

that they ate at her _____. (etbal)

4. Jezebel's story is in the Book of _____.

5. Two idols remind us of Queen _____.

R is for Rebekah

Rebekah said to her son Jacob, "I heard your father speak to your brother Esau, 'Bring me game and prepare for me delicious food, that I may eat it and bless you before the LORD before I die.'

Genesis 27.6-7

Quiz - (See answers in back)

1. Rebekah had two sons: Jacob and _____. (uase)

2. She eavesdropped on her son Esau and his and Jacob's:

a. Uncle   b. housekeeper   c. father

3. His father told Esau to bring food and he would

_____ (lebss) him.

4. Rebekah works out her trick in the Book of

_____.

5. A _____ of stew reminds us of Rebekah.

S is for Samaritan Woman

The woman said to him, 'I know that Messiah is coming' (who is called Christ). 'When he comes, he will proclaim all things to us.' Jesus said to her, 'I am he,* the one who is speaking to you.'
John 4. 25-26

Quiz - (See answers in back)

1. The Samaritan was expecting _____ (sesmiah) to come.

2. The one she was expecting was also called _____ (hircts).

3. Jesus told her "I am he," meaning he was the:
a. Angel   b. Christ   c. Preacher

4. The Samaritan Woman is in the Gospel of _____.

5. The woman who talked to Jesus at the well carried a _____.

T is for Titus

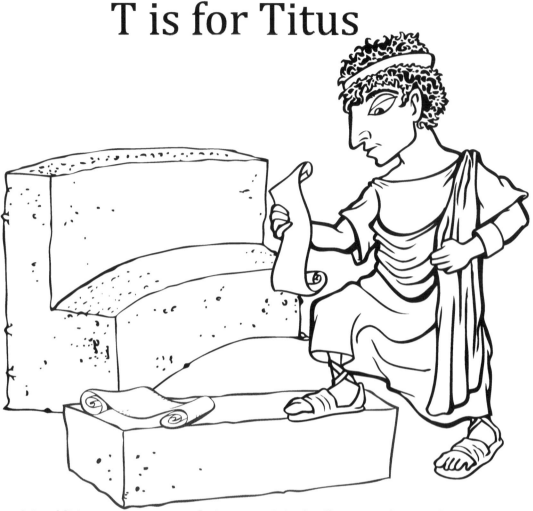

[Paul wrote} In addition to our own consolation, we rejoiced still more at the joy of Titus, because his mind has been set at rest by all of you.

2 Corinthians 7.13

Quiz - (See answers in back)

1. Paul's co-worker, Titus, had been worried about the

Corinthians. Did they make him feel better?   a. Yes   b. No

2. When Paul heard things were going well for Titus, he

_____ (reeciodj)

3. Titus was Paul's only co-worker.   a. True   b. False

4. Paul speaks of Titus' joy in his letter called

_____.

5. The symbol for Titus is the letter to the_____.

U is for United Tribes

Then Jacob called his sons, and said: 'Gather around, that I may tell you what will happen to you in days to come. Assemble and hear, O sons of Jacob; listen to Israel your father.

Genesis 49.1-2

Quiz - (See answers in back)

1. Jacob told his 12 sons to _____ (hergat) around

and listen.

2. He was going to tell them what would happen in the:

a. Village   b. future   c. next county

3. Jacob was also called:

a. Pop Jake   b. Henry   c. Israel

4. Jacob talks to the united tribes (his sons) in the Book of

_____ .

5. The Shield or Star of David is the symbol of the United _____ .

V is for Voice of God

...and a great and strong wind tore into the mountains and broke the rocks in pieces before the LORD, but the LORD was not in the wind; and after the wind an earthquake, but the LORD was not in the earthquake; and after the earthquake a fire, but the LORD was not in the fire; and after the fire a still small voice.

1 Kings 19.11-12 (NKJV)

Quiz - (See answers in back)

1. The wind was so strong, it broke _____ (cksro)

in pieces.

2. God was not in the _____ (qaukeerath)

or the fire.

3. God was heard as a still small _____ (iocev).

4. Elijah hears God's quiet voice in the Book of

_____.

5. An _____reminds us to listen for God's still small voice.

W is for the Woman of Shunem

So whenever [Elisha] passed that way, he would stop there for a meal. [The woman of Shunem] said to her husband, 'Look, I am sure that this man who regularly passes our way is a holy man of God.

2 Kings 4.8-9

Quiz - (See answers in back)

1. The woman lived in a town called _____

(nemsuh).

2. The Prophet Elisha would stop by her house for a:

a. Month   b. meal   c. walking stick

3. She was sure Elisha was a _____ (lyho)

man of God.

4. The Woman of Shunem's story is in the Book of

_____.

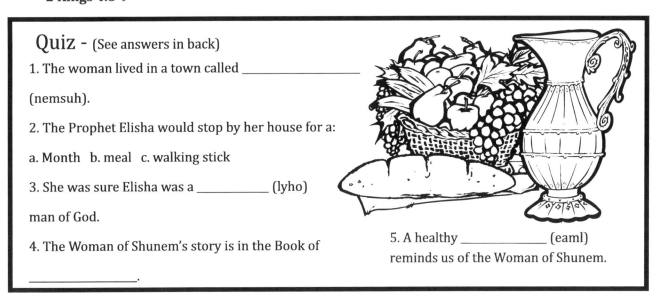

5. A healthy _____ (eaml) reminds us of the Woman of Shunem.

X is for X (Ten) Commandments

Then God spoke all these words: I am the Lord your God, who brought you out of the land of Egypt, out of the house of slavery; you shall have no other gods before me.

Exodus 20.1-2

Quiz - (See answers in back)

1. The Roman letter for the number 10 was:
a. R   b. Y   c. X

2. God's first Commandment was to have no other _____ (gdos).

3. God brought the people out of slavery in _____. (pyteg)

4. The 10 Commandments can be read in the Book of _____.

5. The large letter _____ reminds us of the Ten Commandments.

Y is for Yehudah

'Judah, your brothers shall praise you; your hand shall be on the neck of your enemies; your father's sons shall bow down before you.

Genesis 49.8

Quiz - (See answers in back)

1. The ancient Hebrews would have called Judah _____ (hudhaey)

2. His father Israel told him his brothers would _____ (raiesp) him.

3. Yehudah's brothers would also:
a. bow down   b. leave home   c. forget what their father said

4. This story can be found in the Book of _____.

5. Yehudah's symbol is the_____ of Judah.

Z is for Zechariah

But the angel said to him, 'Do not be afraid, Zechariah, for your prayer has been heard. Your wife Elizabeth will bear you a son, and you will name him John.

Luke 1. 13

Quiz - (See answers in back)

1. The angel told Zechariah not to fear because his

_____ (rayrep) had been heard.

2. Zechariah's wife was named:

a. Miriam   b. Elizabeth   c. Ashley

3. Zechariah was to name his son _____. (hjon)

4. Zechariah's story is in the Gospel of

_____.

5. A tablet with _____ written on it reminds us of Zechariah.

Quiz 'N Color Answers Section 1

Anna
1. 2, Luke
2. fasting
3. prophet
4. Joseph
5. Temple

Barnabas
1. Paul
2. Lord
3. Apostle
4. Walked
5. Sandles

Cornelius
1. Centurion
2. Caesarea
3. Generous
4. Household
5. Helmet

Deborah
1. Judge
2. Palm
3. Lappidoth
4. Ephraim
5. Palm tree

Elizabeth
1. Blamelessly
2. John the Baptist
3. Moses Miriam
4. Luke
5. Shell

Fishers
1. John
2. Fish nets
3. People
4. Follow me
5. Helmet
6. Fish

Gideon
1. Jars torches
      trumpets
2. Judges
3. Understand
4. Look same
5. Trumpet

Huldah
1. Consulted
2. Second Quarter
3. Priests
4. 2 Kings
5. Scrolls

Isaiah
1. God
2. Wolves lambs
3. A child
4. Isaiah
5. Wolf lamb

Joanna
1. Provided
2. Herod
3. Mary Magdalene,
   Susanna
4. Luke
5. Purse

King David
1. Shepherd
2. Stones, sling
3. Goliath
4. 1 Samuel
5. Crown

Lydia
1. Purple
2. Worshipper
3. Acts
4. Thyatira
5. Fabric

Miriam
1. Prophet   Moses
2. Music
3. Exodus
4. With other people
5. Tambourine

Nicodemus
1. Pharisee
2. God
3. The Dark of night
4. Teacher
5. Hood

Onesimus
1. Prison
2. Philemon
3. Child   Father
4. Preaching
5. Slaves

Phoebe
1. Deacon
2. Cenchreae
3. Welcome
4. Romans
5. Scroll

Queen of Sheba
1. Solomon
2. The Lord
3. Hard questions
4. 1 Kings
5. Feathers

Ruth
1. Following
2. People God   God
3. The same home
4. Ruth
5. Wheat (or grain)

Samuel
1. Temple
2. The voice of God
3. Here I am
4. 1 Samuel
5. Coat

Tabitha
1. Disciple
2. Acts of charity
3. Greek
4. Acts
5. Needle

Urriah
1. David
2. Wife
3. Forefront   fighting
4. 2 Samuel
5. Helmet

Visitors
1. Magi
2. Child   Jews
3. Bethlehem
4. Matthew
5. Gifts

Widow
1. Elisha
2. Slaves
3. Prophet
4. 2 Kings
5. Jar (or jug)

Xerxes
1. Xerxes
2. Jews
3. Kingdom
4. Esther
5. Turbin

Yahweh
1. Holy to be spoken
2. The Lord
3. Esther
4. Yahweh
5. Creation (Nature)

Zipporah
1. Zipporah
2. Moab
3. Life
4. Marriage
5. Tablets

Quiz 'N Color Answers Section 2

Abraham
1. Abram
2. House
3. Nation, Blessing
4. Genesis
5. Shepherd

Bathsheba
1. Bathsheba, Solomon
2. King
3. Throne
4. 1 Kings
5. Throne

Caleb
1. Spirit
2. Wholeheartedly
3. Land
4. Numbers
5. Honey

Delilah
1. Bound
2. Strength
3. Hair
4. Judges
5. Scissors

Elijah
1. walking, talking
2. horse
3. Whirlwind
4. Kings
5. Chariot

Flood Family
1. 8
2. Waters, Flood
3. Animals
4. Genesis
5. Rainbow

Gabriel
1. Afraid
2. Jesus
3. Messengers
4. Luke
5. Angel

Hagar
1. Voice
2. Great, Nation
3. Heaven
4. Genesis
5. Eye

Israel
1. Late in life
2. Coat
3. Unhappy
4. Genesis
5. Twins

Jochebed
1. Papyrus
2. Bitumen, pitch
3. Pharaoh
4. Exodus
5. Basket

King Darius
1. Early morning
2. Living
3. Delivered, lions
4. Daniel
5. Lion

Lois
1. Grandmother
2. Eunice
3. Faith
4. Timothy
5. Board (tablet)

Martha
1. Distracted
2. Sister, work
3. Worry
4. Luke
5. Broom

Naomi
1. Restorer
2. Seven, sons
3. Ruth
4. Ruth
5. Branch

Obadiah
1. Eagle
2. Stars
3. Prophet
4. Edom
5. Ink

Priscilla
1. Way, God
2. Aquila
3. Tentmakers
4. Acts
5. Fireplace

Qohelet
1. Season
2. Born, die
3. Pluck it
4. Ecclesiastes
5. Leaf

Rahab
1. King
2. House
3. Land
4. Joshua
5. Red

Sarah
1. Laughed
2. Old
3. Pleasure
4. Genesis
5. Stars

Thomas
1. Jesus
2. Doubt
3. Lord, God
4. Disciples
5. Square

Uzziah
1. Proud
2. Offering
3. False
4. 2 Chronicles
5. broken

Vashti
1. Beauty
2. Command
3. Crown
4. Esther
5. Mirror

Woman Wisdom
1. Wisdom
2. Silver, gold
3. Happy
4. Proverbs
5. Jewels

"X" Cross of St. Andrew
1. John, Jesus
2. Simon Peter
3. Cross
4. Gospels
5. Cross

Young Jesus
1. Jesus
2. 3 days
3. Temple, teachers
4. Luke
5. Steps

Zacchaeus
1. Jesus
2. Stay, house
3. hurried down
4. Luke
5. Tree

Quiz 'N Color Answers Section 3

Abigail
1. Hundred
2. Donkeys
3. Coming after you
4. Samuel
5. Bread

Bezalel
1. Bezalel
2. Divine spirit
3. Gold and wood
4. Exodus
5. Bezalel

Centurion
1. Paralyzed
2. Come and cure him
3. Roof
4. Matthew
5. Centurion

Dinah
1. Leah and Jacob
2. Women
3. Shechem
4. Genesis
5. Dinah's

Eve
1. Snake
2. Middle
3. Eat, touch, die
4. Genesis
5. fruit

Four Daughters
1. Evangelist
2. Married
3. Prophecy
4. Acts
5. Hands

Goliath
1. Philistine
2. Fight
3. Defy
4. 1 Samuel
5. rocks (stones)

Hannah
1. exults
2. exalted
3. praying
4. 1 Samuel
5. coat (robe)

Ishmael
1. Wilderness
2. Egypt
3. Bow
4. Genesis
5. Bow

Jonathan
1. Soul
2. Loved
3. Saul
4. 1 Samuel
5. sword

King Herod
1. Frightened
2. Priests, scribes
3. Messiah
4. Matthew
5. castle (palace)

Leah
1. Two
2. Lovely
3. Graceful, beautiful
4. Genesis
5. Eyes

Mary Magdelene
1. Dawn
2. Earthquake
3. Angel, Heaven
4. Matthew
5. Tomb

Nehemiah
1. Hanani
2. Jerusalem
3. Jews
4. Nehemiah
5. Map

Orphans
1. Pure
2. Widows
3. Unstained
4. James
5. Hands

Puah
1. Midwives
2. God
3. Live
4. Exodus
5. Baby

Queen Jezebel
1. Baal
2. 850
3. Table
4. 1 Kings
5. Jezebel

Rebekah
1. Esau
2. Father
3. Bless
4. Genesis
5. Bowl

Samaritan Woman
1. Messiah
2. Christ
3. Christ
4. John
5. Jar (jug)

Titus
1. Yes
2. Rejoiced
3. False
4. 2 Corinthians
5. Corinthians

United Tribes
1. Gather
2. Future
3. Israel
4. Genesis
5. Tribes

Voice of God
1. Rocks
2. Earthquake
3. Voice
4. 1 Kings
5. Ear

Woman of Shunem
1. Shunem
2. Meal
3. Holy
4. 2 Kings
5. meal

X Commandments
1. X
2. Gods
3. Egypt
4. Exodus
5. X

Yehudah
1. Yahudah
2. Praise
3. Bow down
4. Exodus
5. Lion

Zechariah
1. Prayer
2. Elizabeth
3. John
4. Luke
5. John

Characters & Their Symbols

INSTRUCTIONS:
Draw a line from the character's name to her or his corresponding symbol.

Anna

Barnabas

Cornelius

Deborah

Elizabeth

Fishers (Peter, Andrew, James & John)

Gideon

Huldah

Isaiah

Joanna

King David

Lydia

Miriam

Nicodemus

Onesimus

Phoebe

Queen of Sheba

Ruth

Samuel

Tabitha

Uriah

Visitors (Magi)

Widow (with multiplied oil)

Xerxes

Yahweh

Zipporah

Characters & Their Symbols

INSTRUCTIONS:
Draw a line from the character's name to her or his corresponding symbol.

Abraham

Bathsheba

Caleb

Delilah

Elijah

Flood Family

Gabriel

Hagar

Israel

Jochebed

King Darius

Lois

Martha

Naomi

Obadiah

Priscilla

Qohelet

Rahab

Sarah

Thomas

Uzziah

Queen Vashti

Woman Wisdom

X: Cross of Andrew

Young Jesus

Zacchaeus

Characters & Their Symbols

INSTRUCTIONS:
Draw a line from the character's name to her or his corresponding symbol.

Abigail

Bezalel

Centurion

Dinah

Eve

Four Daughters of Philip

Goliath

Hannah

Ishmael

Jonathan

King Herod,

Leah

Mary Magdalene

Nehemiah

Orphans & Widows

Puah

Queen Jezebel

Rebekah

Samaritan

Titus

United Tribes

Voice of God

Woman of Shunem

X - Ten Commandments

Yahudah

Zechariah.

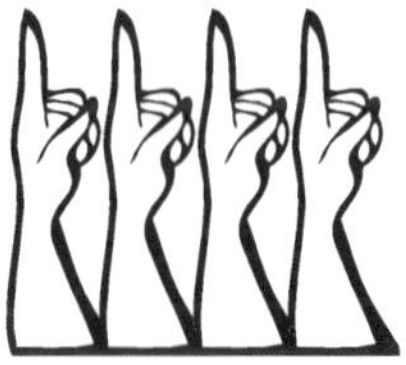

31538123R00052

Made in the USA
Charleston, SC
21 July 2014